MARRIAGE LESSONS

MARRIAGE LESSONS

MARRIAGE LESSONS FOR SINGLES AND MARRIED COUPLES

LENIN WERE

Restoration of the Tent of David

Contents

1 MARRIAGE LESSONS — 1

2 Endorsements — 3

3 Copyright — 5

4 Dedication — 7

5 Foreward — 9

6 Preface — 11

One
MAN SHALL LEAVE HIS FATHER'S HOUSE AND BE UNITED TO HIS WIFE — 14

Two TO OUR SINGLE LADIES	18
Three TO THE MARRIED COUPLES	20
Four MOTHER OF MANY NATIONS	21
Five TAKE ME TO REST LORD	26
Six THE POWER OF TWO IN MARRIAGE RESTORATION	29
Seven HOLY MATRIMONY	33
Eight I MADE A COVENANT WITH MY EYES	36
Nine PURSUIT OF INDEPENDENCE	39
Ten AVOID SEX BEFORE MARRIAGE	41
Eleven MARRIAGE IS NOT A SOLUTION TO LUST	47
Twelve THE REASON BEHIND THE CHASING	53
Thirteen FOUNDATION ISSUES TO DEAL WITH BEFORE MARRIAGE	55
Fourteen BENEFITS OF HOLY MATRIMONY	59

Fifteen
MESSAGE TO OUR SINGLE PARENTS   62

Sixteen
BE CAUTIOUS IN RELATIONSHIPS   64

Seventeen
DON'T WAIT FOR HER IN A DREAM   66

Eighteen
THE GLORY OF A WIFE IS HER HUSBAND   69

Nineteen
GOOD CHARACTER   71

Twenty
ABOUT THE AUTHOR   79

1

MARRIAGE LESSONS

FOR SINGLES AND MARRIED COUPLES.

LENIN O. WERE

2

Endorsements

I recommend this book to everyone, having known the man of God Pastor Lenny at a personal level makes it even easier. I love the simplicity and practicality of it.

Three key chapters that stood out for me, "Mother of many nations" in chapter 4. I like the call to our young women of today to deny self and make the necessary adjustments and sacrifices because nothing good comes easy. The other one is " I made a covenant with my eyes" in chapter 8. I like the element about not just choosing out of physical beauty but inwardly as we are urged in the book of Peter, we shouldn't trust our physical eyes on a critical decision as marriage. Finally is the chapter on "don't wait for her in a dream" chapter 17. This is an eye opener since many young men want to sleep and God to show them who their wife is and that seems like a short cut to me, so this is a good guide to how practical finding your marriage partner is.

Pastor Kelvin Obonyo
Home of Transformation Ministry in Nairobi, Kenya.
Mentor, Life Coach, Event planner and Speaker

Marriage Lessons for singles and married couples is a must - read Christian book covering a wide range of information and advice concerning marriage as an institution ordained by God. Pastor Lenin Were takes readers through personal testimonies out of this book, making the book content easily consistent with life applications.

Mr. Linus Otieno Mathews,
Leader at Restoration of the Tent of David Church. Migori Kenya

Pastor Lenny Were's book is one of the first and best from a young person to inspire and guide the world to anchor marriages on the sanctity of the Lord God, the initiator of the marriage institution. Read this book and save marriages.

Francis Odiyo
Teacher and Teenage Councilor.
Yolanda Daycare Centre, Migori Kenya.

The book **MARRIAGE LESSONS** have a lot of great impacts to the lives of both men and women. The book is destined to shape and groom the behaviors of young men as far as marriage is concerned. The author warns young men from entering marriage before they are fully ready to take the responsibilities.

He warns men from being over dependent on their parents. He is also against the behavior of men being so close to their mothers thereby abandoning their wives in the process. Despite coming from a rich family, the author encourages young men to be industrious by generating their own wealth and this he support by *John 14:2*, and therefore he refers to man as the vision bearer of the home and it is essential for him to have a reliable source of income.

I recommend that the book should be read by men and women who are yet to get married so as they can understand fully what it takes to be in marriage life.

Ibrahim Lumumba Owino
Senior Student , BS Microbiology and Biotechnology.
University of Embu, Kenya.

Copyright

Marriage Lessons, for Singles and Married Couples

Copyright© 2020 by Lenin O Were. All rights reserved.

No part of this book may be reproduced, stored in a retrieval system , or transmitted in any form or by any means - electronic, mechanical, photocopy, recording , or otherwise- without prior written permission of the copyright owner, except by a reviewer who wishes to quote brief passages in connection with the review for inclusion in a magazine, newspaper, or broadcast.

Requests for information should be addressed to:

Restoration of the Tent of David

www.restorationofthetentofdavid.com

pastorlenny@restorationofthetentofdavid.com

Unless otherwise indicated, all scriptures are taken from The Holy Bible, New King James Version. Copyright © 1979, 1980, 1982 by Thomas Nelson, Inc.

BOOK ISBN: 978-1-7345121-1-3
EBOOK ISBN: 978-1-7345121-0-6

FOR MORE INFORMATION ON STREAMS AND OTHER MATERIALS,

CALL 1.773.793.6628 (U.S.A)

4

Dedication

I dedicate this book to my beloved wife Jacinter Lenin, the wife of my youth and the beautiful gift God gave to me. I also dedicate it to my son David Lenin that he will learn and grow in the will of God and honor the institution of marriage as God designed it.

My final dedication is to the family of Restoration of the Tent of David. Members of this family keeps me going as I gear towards the vision of God for His House.

Foreword

The intention of the book is to heal, build, and strengthen marriages in a new world in which the institution of marriage faces numerous challenges that threaten its very survival, even within the Christian context. Given the strategic importance of marriage and family as the foundation of the church, the community, and the nation, the book places high premium, and rightly so, on God's principles and values that are intended to nurture and protect marriage, especially among Christians.

The author effectively uses his personal testimony derived from his background, in which his own parents went through divorce, to warn against the dangers of unresolved concerns and family rifts. He them proceeds to delve into various themes of the book in order to empower his readers. In Chapter 1 he uses the Genesis 2:24 lesson of "leaving and cleaving" to explain the importance of maturity before marriage. It is an idea that needs to be deeply cultivated among premarital youth so as to develop stronger marriages.

The author dedicates Chapter 2 to single ladies and uses the biblical example of Rachael to teach the virtue of chastity and honor before marriage. In Chapter 3, married couples are advised to dedicate themselves to deepening the relationship with their spouse. Chapter 4 specifically addresses mothers and the concept of motherhood as God planned it. Chapter 5 urges young men to rest and trust God, rather than spend time and energy in searching for a partner. Chapter 6 focuses on restoration whenever failure occurs and how to move forward despite the challenges that may arise in marriage.

Chapter 7 places emphasis on holiness and honoring God in the marriage, rather than planning only for the glamour of the wedding. Chapter 8 advises those who intend to enter into marriage to look beyond outer beauty or physical attraction, and to be able to appreciate more the virtues and inner qualities found in a potential partner. Three serious warning follow each other: Chapter 9 warns against the contemporary tendency of individuals in a marriage seeking independent ways of fulfilling their desires, without involving the other; Chapter 10 which teaches the virtue of purity before marriage; and Chapter 11 warns against misconceiving marriage to be a solution for lust.

Attraction is analyzed in Chapter 12 which also helps individuals understand what causes them to "chase after" the other person. There are foundational issues that need to be faced and discussed before marriage, and the author discusses them in Chapter 13, just before having a deeper discussion in Chapter 14 of what holy matrimony is all about. Chapter 15 handles the sensitive issue of single parenting, while Chapter 16 provides the reader with caution on relationships outside the marriage. Chapter 17 helps a young man on the way to approach the lady, instead of simply waiting in the spiritual realm. The husband as the glory of the wife is covered in Chapter 18, before the book spends its last chapter on how good character builds a marriage and a family.

The book is timely, relevant, and suitable for Christians in Bible-believing churches before and during marriages. It is both educative and corrective. Its greatest strength lies in the careful application of biblical passages in the teaching of its powerful lessons. I would implore all couples, married and unmarried, to read it and apply its lessons.

Tom J. Obengo, PhD
Senior Lecturer, Moffat College, Kijabe.

6

Preface

I want to thank God for this opportunity for his grace to enable me to write this book. I believe God will use this book to heal, build and strengthen many marriages to rise to fulfill their God given mandate on earth.

We live in a time where marriages are under heavy attacks of the enemy across the nations. The enemy knows why God cherishes marriage as the first institution He ever created on earth. Marriage is powerful for the future of the nation's depend on the children we raise in our homes.

Having grown and raised in a broken home, the Lord enabled me to have various experiences that left many impressions on me as I grew up. Many impressions have become lifelong lessons that have led to the writing of this book. I often say that I grew up as an orphan though I was not one. Both my parents were alive, but I never had an opportunity to grow with them in the same house as a child.

There are many a times, filled with pain and sorrow, blamed God for the cause of my parent's separation. I suffered rejection as I walked from one home to another looking for acceptance and love. I desired that kind of love a child could receive from both parents, but it was hard to get it. I always yearned for a place I could call home but did not find one.

With a broken heart, one day after coming to the knowledge of Jesus Christ as my personal Savior, I demanded answers from God concerning my parent's separation. One evening, in High School, I open the scriptures to find answers about this. The Lord led me to the Book of Isaiah. The Lord spoke to my heart from this Book that He came to rescue my parent's marriage, but nobody heeded his help. He made me understand that He has enough power to save, to heal and to deliver but our lack of faith in him is what prevent Him from doing what He desire to do. He made me understand that when He called no one answered. It is that moment I knew that God is always near to save us from any danger or anything that will cause us pain, but we often fail to listen to that still small voice during great turmoil.

Isaiah 50: 1 Thus says the Lord: "Where is the certificate of your mother's divorce, Whom I have put away? Or which of My creditors is it to whom I have sold you? For your iniquities you have sold yourselves, And for your transgressions your mother has been put away. 2 Why, when I came, was there no man? Why, when I called, was there none to answer? Is My hand shortened at all that it cannot redeem? Or have I no power to deliver? Indeed with My rebuke I dry up the sea, I make the rivers a wilderness; Their fish stink because there is no water And die of thirst. 3 I clothe the heavens with blackness, And I make sackcloth their covering." (NKJ)

These scriptures opened the door of my healing process as a child who passed through the pain of divorce of his parents. I often say that when it comes to divorce, children often suffer the most than adults. This is one of the major reasons why God hate divorce. Divorce leaves serious injuries both on children and couples that are hard to heal.

I thank God for His Agape love and the love that flows from Calvary that healed my heart. When God healed my heart, I considered what my parents went through as learning lessons. I listened to both side of the stories of what led to their separations, coupled with the Word of God, gave me great insight even to the writing of this book.

As a young person in his service before I got married to my wife, the Lord led me to pray and counsel many marriages at the brick of divorce and God healed those marriages and those couples still live together. God started using me in this ministry of marriage before I even got married myself. I witnessed people who have been married for years coming to me for marriage counseling and prayer. This humbled me why God could do this. Then I learnt that one of the ministries that Jesus has given me is to restore marriages back to the will of God. I strongly believe that this is one of the core ministries of my Pastoral calling in the church.

I prayed to God never to repeat my parent's mistakes. I prayed for his wisdom, understanding and counsel even to the wife He will give me. I wanted my life to be different for I knew that deep in my heart God made marriage to work.

This book carries stories and teachings that are part of this journey of the power of God in marriage. How we can do great things and achieve much when we understand the original plan of God for creating marriage. When things get difficult, when people miss direction, they go back to the original plan and blueprint. This book returns us back to the mind of God on the institution that He cherished to fulfill His will and Mandate on earth.

Pastor Lenny Were
Founder
Restoration of the Tent of David.

One

MAN SHALL LEAVE HIS FATHER'S HOUSE AND BE UNITED TO HIS WIFE

The Lord put in my heart to turn my focus to teachings concerning marriage and relationship leading to marriage.

For this reason, I will have to become obedient and heed to the direction of God. Let us start with this scripture:

Genesis 2:24 Therefore a man shall leave his father and his mother and hold fast to his wife, and they shall become one flesh.

The first requirement of entering marriage is maturity. Yes, the man getting married must be mature enough to be able to sustain himself without the help of his parents. He must be mature enough to make his decision without involving the parent, he must be mature enough to run his own household, he must be mature enough even financially to run his own house without the help of the parents.

We see when God calls man to marriage, the first instruction is that he must leave his father's house. Oh, but today we live in a generation that brings their so-called girlfriends in their parents' house and even impregnate them there. What a shame! You are a young man, you are not able even to take care of yourself, how shall you be able to take care of your wife? You still sleep under your parents' house because you can't afford to live on your own, but in your mind, you want to get married. This is a no according to the first principle of God.

Yes, this man getting married cannot be a baby mama, he must be mature enough and have capability to sustain himself without the help of the parents.

We see a perfect example in the life of Jesus. Jesus says that in his Father's house there are many mansions, but He still goes to prepare a place for His Bride. It doesn't matter how rich your parents are, as a man you have a responsibility to prepare a place for your wife to come and stay with you.

As a man, the only way you will be able to secure the position of your wife is to find a place for her you can call your own. With this, it will be difficult for the in laws to become a threat to your marriage. Many marriages are breaking today not because of the inward pressure of the couples, but because of the interference of the in laws or pressure from outside.

John 14:2 In My Father's house are many mansions; if it were not so, I would have told you. I go to prepare a place for you. (NKJ)

The man must find himself work as the vision bearer of the home. God gave man work first before He gave him a wife. It was the work that the man already had which increased the need of a helper. It is important for our single ladies to identify a man who already have work. They already have purpose in life and goals to pursue. As a young lady you will need to pray for wisdom and direction of God to see if the vision of the man will be able to accommodate your vision and things you would like to pursue in life. Don't marry a man thinking you will be able to change what they like to what you like or their pursuit in life to your pursuit.

Don't marry him if you are not willing to join his vision. If the two are going different path, then it is not wise to get married. Message to our young single women. If you can't submit to his vision, call and purpose in life, you won't be able to submit to him as the head of the house. Therefore make sure before you join your hands in marriage that the man is the right man for you.

The second, the man must be willing to cling to his wife. When two people come together to get married are often challenged with various backgrounds. This background will determine their character and way of life. We often grow very attached to our parents and siblings, but a time comes where God want you to cling to your wife. In other words, make her the most important person in your life after God. There is tendency where men fail to stand with their wife when there is a dispute between their wife with either their parents or someone from outside. It is important for a man to know that standing with the wife is very key to perfect marriage life. God calls us to cling to our wife and bear responsibility of raising godly offspring's in a happy home.

Now it is your wife the Lord is saying you should cling to, not your parents, not your brothers, not your sisters, not your friends but your wife. You will have to be able to defend her against negative attacks from the in laws. The shocking part is this, even when your wife may have flaws, or done something that is wrong that is upsetting other people, the Lord still calls you to stand with her even when she will be wrong in some circumstances and help her overcome.

It is the responsibility of the man to hold first to his wife and not to let her go. Challenges may come in the marriage, but the man must remember that God hold him responsible to cling first to his wife. The faith of the wife may lack but still God calls the man to hold first to his wife, the wife may be inadequate in character, but God still hold the man to hold first to his wife. Today, there are men who have forgotten this responsibility and principle, instead of holding first to the wife they chose themselves, they are ever looking for minor mistakes on their wives to attack them on. They are ever looking for ways to bring problems. They are not able to stand and defend their wives in the eyes of the world. Yes, the man is called to defend his wife in the negative eyes of the world and the people in his circles in Jesus Mighty Name. Amen.

The third, become one flesh. Marriage involve interlinks of emotions, sex and soul. When couples become one, it means they share their bodies together. Sex is not a tool of just satisfying lust of the flesh but a way of discovering your partner. It is through sex in marriage where you get to know the deeper emotions, thoughts and feelings that are embedded in your partner. You come to a level of knowing when they are sad, disappointed with something, troubled, happy or annoyed. When couples deny themselves conjugal rights, the further they grow away in their relationship. God meant sex as a way of procreation and as an expression of love and feeling between couples. It is sex that unites the bond between couples in marriage.

1 Corinthians 7:3

Let the husband render to his wife the affection due her, and likewise also the wife to her husband. (NKJ)

Two

TO OUR SINGLE LADIES

Genesis 29:12 And Jacob told Rachel that he was her father's relative and that he was Rebekah's son. So she ran and told her father. (NKJ)

Where is the Rachael of our time that when a man approaches her, she run to her father? They quickly report the matter to their father. Saying, "father, I met this strange man at the well who had interest on me. Father you know you are always my role model, but this stranger even kissed me, I had to report it to you."

Many of our single ladies today when approached with a man, end up in a French fry restaurant and finally in a man's bedroom. Some were approached in a bar, party, club, school and ended up in a one-night stand. They woke up only to realize they slept on somebody's bed or raped.

Some were approached and ended up with a married man, only later to realize they have become serious home breakers.

Some were approached and ended up in cohabitation, living with a man as if married and yet not married but enjoying every right of married couples.

Some were approached and the only nice gift they returned to the father at home is a child out of wedlock.

Where are the Rachael's, children who have been raised with dignity and honor, children who will not sell their body for a gift or chicken on a French fry?

Yes, where are the Rachel's; women who respect and honor themselves, yes young ladies from functioning families who understands order and knows that there are cruel men outside there who cannot be trusted?

To single ladies reading this book, just know that just as cheaply found, shall you be cheaply left. People tend to value things they sweat to get. If you are just the easy going who is easily swayed here and there to lose you virginity in the name of love , you are in a hot trouble , for you will see that man walking around with another lady in your own eyes after defiling you. Always identify a father or spiritual parent and introduce your relationship early enough to them for direction and spiritual guidance. It is good for a man to find you anchored on a father's relationship. A man will be able to respect you knowing that they didn't just meet you on the streets but from a functioning home and proper leadership.

Three

TO THE MARRIED COUPLES

To the married couples, let none be your best friend except your spouse. For you are supposed to be one, joined in spirit and in body.

So, don't lie to yourself by putting someone else to be your best friend. Let your husband or your wife be your best friend. Many marriages are breaking because couples spend too much time with their so called "best friends", while they are having problems relating with their spouses at home.

You don't have time for your wife or husband, but you spend too much time with your so-called best friend.

Yes, only the truth will set you free. Make it your priority to make your spouse your best friend.

Overcome the barriers that are between you and work it out until you become comfortable with your spouse in normal to normal day conversations.

Proverbs 5:18 Let your fountain be blessed, And rejoice with the wife of your youth. (NKJ)

Four

MOTHER OF MANY NATIONS

Genesis 17:16 And I will bless her and also give you a son by her; then I will bless her, and she shall be a mother of nations; kings of peoples shall be from her. (NKJ)

You are a young lady and you want God to use you for the glory of His Kingdom. You are a lady and you feel the calling of God to the Ministry.

The Bible says that Sarah became a mother of many nations. The nations of the earth today need mothers but where are they? How can they become mothers of many nations when they are chasing after the world?

You cannot become a mother of many nations without self-denial. A mother is the one that will always eat the last plate after the children are full. She eats the scrambles just to make sure the hungry children are fed.

We have many hungry children of our generation that needs to be fed.

They need to be told beauty is not in the external appearance but the inward work of God

1 Peter 3:3 Do not let your adornment be merely outward—arranging the hair, wearing gold, or putting on fine apparel— 4 rather let it be the hidden person of the heart, with the incorruptible beauty of a gentle and quiet spirit, which is very precious in the sight of God. 5 For in this manner, in former times, the holy women who trusted in God also adorned themselves, being submissive to their own husbands, 6 as Sarah obeyed Abraham, calling him lord, whose daughters you are if you do good and are not afraid with any terror. (NKJ)

They need to be told to first respect themselves before learning to respect others , they need to be told what integrity is and what virtue is, they need to be told what it is to be a godly woman , they need to be told what makes a woman of the house , they need to be told is not amount of makeup you put which makes you beautiful but the time you spend with God on your knees.

We have a hungry generation their hearts are thirsty, and they are feeding their thirsts with the garbage of this world. These are led to teenage pregnancies, children raised in broken families, children raising children when they are children themselves, irresponsible men who don't want to take responsibility of their own actions and there is an outcry in the nations.

There is a cry for consolation, there is a cry in need of love, there is a cry for a mother. Today we have mothers who are hungrier than their children. They are more obsessed with the world than their children are. They have children but still want to be called 'miss'. They are aging but they still wish to be young. They are becoming elderly, but they wish they were youths. They live as if they are missing their youths:

They are number one in miniskirts together with their children.

They are number one in disobedience to the husband or authority God has given them as the children follow along.

They are number one in low self-esteem which is coupled with the way they behave.

They are number one in lavishness and excessive pleasures and material things of this world.

They spend more time on a mirror doing makeups even when they are married. They still want to look attractive to some young men outside there besides their husband.

They are wily of heart and number one leading their children to destructions. They tell their children not to smoke but they smoke, they tell their children not to drink alcohol, but they drink, they tell their children not to play with men, but they keep on exchanging men and boyfriends.

They are not home makers. They have no time to cook for the family. Therefore, children are fed with most unhealthy food from the restaurant and children walk around obese. For the mother is too busy, she doesn't know how to wash the utensils, she doesn't know how to clean the house, she doesn't know how to cook but she knows career. As she pursues career the family is left broken into pieces.

Titus 2:3 the older women likewise, that they be reverent in behavior, not slanderers, not given to much wine, teachers of good things 4 that they admonish the young women to love their husbands, to love their children, 5 to be discreet, chaste, homemakers, good, obedient to their own husbands, that the word of God may not be blasphemed.(NKJ)

She has no time to teach her children the way of truth. She has no time to seat down with a daughter and teach her how to become a woman for she isn't one in the first place. If she still feels she is a miss, then how will she teach her daughter to become a woman?

What does it mean that Sarah became a mother of many nations? It means that Sarah taught the nations of the earth what it takes to be a woman, what it takes to be a mother:

A mother is the one seating next to the husband helping the husband make wise decisions in life.

A mother's life is spent in discipline for they won't waste their money on unnecessary things but to make sure the children are taken care of.

A mother is a protector, Sarah protected Isaac from the grip of Ishmael. There are many mothers today that have abandoned their children, some have aborted their children, some are in the process of committing abortion, and some don't just protect their children against any harm. When they see their children accompanied with notorious groups, they don't give a warning, is the reason many mothers are the one burying their children today instead of their children burying them in old age.

A mother understand respect to the authority God has given her. Sarah understood her place in the house was second to her husband. She called her husband 'lord'. How many women can call their husbands 'lord' today? Instead many think their husbands are rival mate. They fight daily for equal power in the house , they want to outdo their husbands they are no longer a companion but a rival.
To our women , God did not call you to be a rival to your husband but a helper and companion . Does your husband feel lonely because you are too busy? Then make time for him so that loneliness may not be filled with a prostitute in a hotel; for man's loneliness was called to be filled with his wife, that is why the Bible says God saw man lonely and therefore needed a companion. Don't be too busy not to spend time with your husband.

1 Peter 3:5 For in this manner, in former times, the holy women who trusted in God also adorned themselves, being submissive to their own husbands, 6 as Sarah obeyed Abraham, calling him lord, whose daughters you are if you do good and are not afraid with any terror. (NKJ)

A mother teaches younger generation what it is to be mother. But how can they teach them when they themselves are not one. There are mothers today jumping on the clubs as they have left the responsibility of the child in the hands of grandparents. They have no time for their children. We have many of our young ladies some are getting married some aspire to get married, but they don't know what it takes to be a wife. When they get married, they end up making huge mess of their lives for they don't know what it is to be a mother, what it is to be wife for they were never taught.

Proverbs 18:22 He who finds a wife finds a good thing, And obtains favor from the LORD. (NKJ)

Five

TAKE ME TO REST LORD

One of the most amazing messages we may contradict. When Adam was in the beautiful Garden of Eden God had given him. One day, he begun to realize he was the only animal without a company. I can imagine it took many years for Adam to walk all along naming every animal. Any animal he named; he could recognize that they were of the same kind. But why couldn't he find his own companion like the rest of the animals?

Gene2: 20 So Adam gave names to all cattle, to the birds of the air, and to every beast of the field. But for Adam there was not found a helper comparable to him. (NKJ)

Reason, he was still searching. The moment Adam forgot all his problems and went to sleep is the moment God took his time to create the bone of his bone and the flesh of his flesh.

Genesis 2:23 And Adam said: "This is now bone of my bones And flesh of my flesh; She shall be called Woman, Because she was taken out of Man." 24

Therefore a man shall leave his father and mother and be joined to his wife, and they shall become one flesh. 25 And they were both naked, the man and his wife, and were not ashamed. (NKJ)

Brothers and sisters in Christ, may we go to rest that the Lord may take over. The moment we spend on searching we can spend on glorifying the Kingdom of God and preparing to be the beautiful maiden of our Lord Jesus. May we spend time up building our faith that we may reach the stature of our Lord and Christ who in his youth no one ever desired even His face. The book of Isaiah says that he never had a good face that men could admire. He was so ugly to the point that even men turned their face on him, then what about the ladies? Nothing good could be seen in our Lord Jesus, nothing good could His generation admire of him.

Isaiah 53:2 For He shall grow up before Him as a tender plant, And as a root out of dry ground. He has no form or comeliness; And when we see Him, There is no beauty that we should desire Him. (NKJ)

An advent youth of his age who was majorly interested in being in the house of God and studying the scriptures with the elders of the temple. A son who became a bother to his brothers and sisters just because of his passion for God and his hour spent in the speaking of the word of God. This was our Lord Jesus, our perfect example.

Youth Ministry cannot progress in the church because many have lost the heavenly focus to earthly focus, who is going to marry who, who is in a relationship with who blah! blah! blah! These have now become a milestone in the house of God. For men who are single learn to wait on the Lord in prayer, to single ladies in the church, strive to be the true Bride of Jesus Christ, first make the best to be the Bride of Christ that will give you eternal life. Let nothing make you lose focus on your Lord Jesus, in his house there is plenty, he has in store for you the right man he purposes for you from the foundation of the world. But it calls for diligence and waiting. Stop banging here and there thinking you are left behind. Did Jesus say the first will be the last and the last will be the first? Concentrate in the Master and his service the rest leave unto the Lord. May we go to rest us we allow God to work in our lives and to find the true partners he has designed for us.

Genesis 2: 21 And the Lord God caused a deep sleep to fall on Adam, and he slept; and He took one of his ribs, and closed up the flesh in its place. 22 Then the rib which the Lord God had taken from man He made into a woman, and He brought her to the man. (NKJ)

Six

THE POWER OF TWO IN MARRIAGE RESTORATION

The importance of marriage is not to find a perfect person but to find somebody who will be able to stand with you and pick you up when you fall.

If your spouse has compromised or fall, is not enough reason to start murmuring and quarreling, it is the time for you to go on your knees and pray for them to rise.

If your spouse has fallen, it is not enough reason to fall also. For if both falls, who will pick another up?

You will hear somebody complaining he or she was the first one to cheat.

Doing wrong in the name of finding wrong in your spouse add up to nothing but more chaos.

If one is standing, the possibility of the other rising is high but if both fall then that marriage will come to an end.

These is why marriage is about companionship and the oneness of marriage will cause the other one to be upright.

That is what the devil doesn't want you to know, the devil wants you to focus on the wrong than possibility of restoration.

There is nothing too hard for the Lord. Men stand before the presence of God on behalf of your legally wedded wife. Stand before the Almighty God and no matter the shake and the twist of Satan in your wife, nothing will happen, and the Lord will bring her back to her place.

Women stand before the presence of God before your legally wedded husband , no matter the shake of any woman outside there, the spirit of your husband will only rest at home.

And it is not a matter of many words that can win your husband but the power of love . Love will break every hard shell; love will level every mountain between you.

> *1 Peter 3: Wives, likewise, be submissive to your own husbands, that even if some do not obey the word, they, without a word, may be won by the conduct of their wives (NKJ)*

Therefore, stop complaining and see beyond what Satan want you to see and pray that your husband will rise to his priestly duty in the house. No matter your knowledge and growth in Christ as a wife, never forget God has called your husband to be the priest of the family. Don't try to take his office but trust God for the better.

> *Ecclesiastes 4 :11 Again, if two lie down together, they will keep warm; But how can one be warm alone? 12 Though one may be overpowered by another, two can withstand him. And a threefold cord is not quickly broken.*
> *(NKJ)*

Marriage involves three entities that is: God, man and his wife. These three entities are what makes the threefold the above book of Ecclesiastes talk about. If two can resist the evil one, how much more can they do when God is at the center of their marriage? It is very important to consider God in your marriage. Before you settle into marriage life, it is important to involve God in the process and to seek for His will and guidance.

The will of God for your marriage is for you to find a believing husband or wife. You are single and trusting God for a marriage partner, do not lower the standard of finding a partner who loves God and fears the Lord. Many believing partner often compromise when it comes to this principle. It is important to know that what God never started it be difficult to maintain. God is the author of marriage and He made marriage to work. For this reason, it is important to involve the author of marriage when you start your relationship. Make sure you are not equally yoked with a non-believer. Don't marry someone thinking you will be able to convert them to Christ. If Christ can't draw them to Himself, you won't be able to draw them to Christ. Be careful when you meet a man or a woman who starts developing interest of the church because of their desire to want to marry you. Make sure that this person is born again, and they love God with their lives. Many people change once they feel they have acquired their goal of marrying you. They will stop going to church with you and start behaving awkward.

> *2 Corinthians 6:14 Do not be unequally yoked together with unbelievers. For what fellowship has righteousness with lawlessness? And what communion has light with darkness? And what accord has Christ with Belial? Or what part has a believer with an unbeliever? 16 And what agreement has the temple of God with idols? For you are the temple of the living God. As God has said: "I will dwell in them And walk among them. I will be their God, And they shall be My people." (NKJ)*

Consider having a wedding for your marriage very highly. Wedding do not only involve vows between the two of you but also God. You are vowing before God in the presence of His servant who represents Him on earth. In other words, you are bringing your marriage to be acknowledged and registered in heaven. There are many marriages that are not registered in heaven as marriage because of failure to follow the protocol of God. Seek for the blessing that comes from the altar when you have a wedding before God. Therefore, the Bibles says whoever finds a wife, find a good thing and obtains favor from God. There is favor that comes to a man when he gets married before God. In other words, there are blessings that God has proportioned only to the married man.

Having a wedding will also seal your marriage before God. The Bible says; whatever God has put together let no man put asunder. This will be a powerful tool to defend your marriage against all odds in the future. You need heaven backup to counter the challenges that will come in the marriage life. You need God at the center of everything to guide you through the process and help the two of you in the most difficult times of your marriage life. You will need the power of the Word of God to keep you strong together to stand against the wiles of the enemy.

Mark 10: 9 Therefore what God has joined together, let not man separate. (NKJ)

Matthew 19:6 So then, they are no longer two but one flesh. Therefore what God has joined together, let not man separate. (NKJ)

Seven

HOLY MATRIMONY

It is not how big your wedding is that count for your marriage. You may have a big celebration and lose out on the grace of marriage. Many have had the celebration part of it but failed to obtain the grace. Don't strive much for celebration at the expense of grace. Make sure your marriage honors God. Follow the right protocol to reach there. Short cuts are costly.

Our young men and women don't live together first before joining hands in marriage at the altar. That's called fornication. Don't defile the woman first before bringing her to the altar for marriage, you may invoke God's curses.

Marriage is supposed to be Holy Matrimony therefore the process must be holy. Two sanctified people needs to come to the altar to get married. But if unfaithful people, who have been living in sin and lost their chastity coming together for marriage can provoke God's curse. You may have the celebration, but you will miss out on the grace that the Lord Himself supplies in marriages that honors Him.

You may make a big celebration in the name of a wedding for friends, relatives and so on but fails to obtain grace from God. Remember friends and relatives will not live together with you only God in your midst can help you.

The Bible says let what God has put together, let no man put asunder. In other words, let no man separate. God will put His signature in that marriage, meaning He will defend that marriage to stand for His Glory by His grace.

Strive to obtain the blessing at the altar at all cost by putting God at the center of everything.

Psalm 11:3

if the foundations are destroyed, what can the righteous do? (NKJ)

Let the foundation of your marriage honor God from the beginning of your relationship. Building on the wrong foundation will be costly with time. If the two of you have been living together , give room for separation , sanctification and a sincere repentance before joining hands at the altar.

God never meant marriage to take the back door ; where people defile themselves first before joining hands at the altar . This is one of the number one reasons why many marriages are failing in our generation. If you choose to do it your way but not God's way, God will not be part of it. Involve God in the process.

To our ladies, run for your life if a man has intent of defiling you before marriage in the name of love. That man doesn't love you and it is the time to quit.

Run for your life when a man tells you that you need to live together to get to know one another before marriage , that is deception from the pit of darkness , for what makes a marriage works is the Holy foundation it has in Christ
Jesus.
Anything built under rottenness of fornication won't prosper and will come with great regrets in life . Us as human beings we are also limited in our knowledge and ability, it is not about us it is about God making it work.

A man accessing you before marriage will destroy your dignity and integrity and that man will never be able to give you proper respect in life. Protect what need to be protected don't open your legs anyhow. The easy you open it the easy you will be treated.

Eight

I MADE A COVENANT WITH MY EYES

Job 31:1 "I have made a covenant with my eyes; Why then should I look upon a young woman? (KJV)

It is only in marriage where you don't have an excuse that I made a mistake. Why? Because you had time to choose. He or she was your choice. You chose her or him among many. You selected the person out of all that is in the world to be one with that person.

Therefore, marriage calls for careful decision making:

Don't rush into marriage when you are not ready for it.

Don't get married because of your parents or relatives.

Let no one force you to marry anyone.

Let it be your soul decision making process to whoever you choose to marry.

Spend time with God to lead your path in choosing the right partner for your life. Spend more time at the feet of Christ than on bars, clubs, parties, Facebook, church and the streets looking for a partner. For unless the Lord build the house, then the builders build it in vain.

Do not be deceived by appearance and physical beauty when it comes to marriage. For physical beauty cannot keep a house but only the beauty from the inside through the working of the Cross in somebody's life. Only this kind of beauty is adorable and sustainable. There are people who married a beauty they find hard to live with. Why? Because the inside is ugly! And their lives are miserable in marriage.

Proverbs 31:30 Charm is deceitful and beauty is passing, But a woman who fears the LORD, she shall be praised. (NKJ)

Tell God to sharpen your eyes when you choose a life partner. First, you need to ask yourself can you live with the person's weakness and strength? Are you attracted to them because of what they have or because the two of you share a common vision and goals in life?

To our young ladies who are born again, strong in the Spirit and feels a calling of God in the Ministry, do not make a mistake of marrying somebody who is a spiritual infant compared to you. Your husband **MUST** be spiritually steadfast than you are. I know these sounds strange to some. Your husband is called to be the priest of the Family, the bread winner, the one who will feed the family with the Bread of Heaven (the Word of God). If you are stronger spiritually than your husband, then contention will be in that house.

These is why many women are leaving their husband at home to open their own Ministry and churches, not knowing they are supposed to work under their husband as the high priest of the family. The husband is the one to open the Ministry, the wife is supposed to work together with him in the vineyard.

If you make a mistake of marrying a man with no interest in serving God yet you have ,then that is a big trouble !

The Bible says, you husbands love your wife has Christ loved the church by washing her with the Word of God.

Ephesians 5: 25 Husbands, love your wives, just as Christ also loved the church and gave Himself for her, 26 that He might sanctify and cleanse her with the washing of water by the word, 27 that He might present her to Him-

self a glorious church, not having spot or wrinkle or any such thing, but that she should be holy and without blemish. 28 So husbands ought to love their own wives as their own bodies; he who loves his wife loves himself. 29 For no one ever hated his own flesh, but nourishes and cherishes it, just as the Lord does the church. 30 For we are members of His body, of His flesh and of His bones. (NKJ)

It is the husband that is supposed to wash the wife with the Word of God. It is the responsibility of the husband to teach the wife the Word of the Living God. It is their mandate to set godly rules and guidelines for the family.

No matter how spiritual you are as a wife; the place of your husband is to bring the Word at home.

Eve made the biggest mistake because she went and ate another food God did not give her husband. If you are a wife and you eat from other sources spiritually which your husband doesn't eat or have never eaten, that house will not have true peace of God.

Therefore, our young ladies considering getting married, think about these facts. If you look at the man, can you learn something from him? Can you be submissive to that person to teach you the Word of God? Do you respect him enough to be the head of your household and the children God will give you? If the answer of the above questions is no, then reconsider your decision.

Nine

PURSUIT OF INDEPENDENCE

Marriage as God planned and ordained was meant for two people, coming together , to work together and form a family and accomplish the purpose and the will of God for their lives together and for them to be one both in spirit, mind and in body .

But the enemy has really got hold of many people with deception. One deception is the spirit of striving to be independent on your own, so you stand for yourself and not see the need of your husband or wife. If that was the case, why did the two of you got married in the first place? If you thought you could do things on your own, achieve your success on your own , raise your children on your own and live your own selfish lifestyle, then there was no need of the two of you getting married .

Many have found themselves in dilemma in marriage when they thought all they need was to be independent on their own. After accomplishing the spirit of independence, they lost their partner and now their lives are more miserable than before.

They thought they could do it on their own without the help of their partner through success in career or education but they forgot there are somethings that are important than success in career or education , yes unity between couples, the love of God that binds them together , the common ordained authority from the head and so on .

If you miss the above, you will live a life of regrets the rest of your life and you will start blaming others for your misfortunes. These is why many people are not happy in their marriage, marriage has become a millstone and the partner has become a headache to endure every day. Today many are just living for the sake of the covenant they made but they lost the meaning of the covenant of marriage. They became empty in the pursuit of independence; they lost the purpose why they got married.

Today, many couples even sleep in two different bedrooms, they can't stand sleeping together on the same bed, yet the Bible says when two sleep together they keep each other warm. Selfishness took hold of them; pride had a great advantage of their lives and the devil sat upon their head and disrespect of authority and of each other took hold of them.

Do not let your pride, arrogance, selfishness, lack of respect to your partner or authority of man as the head of the house steal from you the joy and happiness of marriage.

I thank God for happy married couples today years down their marriage life and I pray for those unhappy couples whom marriage has become a millstone to overcome , have become a prison in which they are locked and have become a headache which they have to endure.

Ten

AVOID SEX BEFORE MARRIAGE

There is something the Lord put a curse on, "sex before marriage". The Lord meant sex to be fulfilling only in marriage out of that it is destructive and have huge consequences! To the youths who are outside there, don't go with the peer pressure to go and taste what God has put an edge on. The fruit may seem lucrative, pleasant, luring, lovely, adorable but inside it is bitter than death.

Peers may talk how great their experience are, but they don't talk how miserable their lives have become! God put a restriction on the garden of Eden, for Adam and Eve not to eat of the fruit at the middle of the garden, but because the fruit in the garden had a tension of its own, with good appearance and seem good for eating, Eve decided to have a taste and the result came to a fall of all humanity. This also goes to fornication, sex before marriage, where the youths have gotten themselves indulged until they have lost themselves, some have even lost their minds. Some have gone deep to the extent they have forgotten who they are, have become whores, homosexuals, lesbians and all manner of filthy lifestyles stack at the teeth of the devil. The devil now has full claim over their lives because they ate what God had forbidden.

The devil will always tie people when they become disobedience to the Lord's command.

Sex before marriage leads to the following:

1.
Sex addiction and slavery to sin. You become a slave to sex, and this will lead you to sexual acts now with even many partners and many have ended up getting HIV/AIDS in this way.

John 8:34

Jesus answered them, "Most assuredly, I say to you, whoever commits sin is a slave of sin. (NKJ)

Romans 6:16

Do you not know that to whom you present yourselves slaves to obey, you are that one's slaves whom you obey, whether of sin leading to death, or of obedience leading to righteousness? (NKJ)

2. Filthy mind and corrupt conscious.
3. Guilty conscious towards God.
4. Separation from the presence of God, where the individual immediately start to withdraw from the presence of God. They can even stop going to church or meeting with brethren.
5. Withdrawal of the Holy Spirit. The Spirit of the Lord will leave that temple, for the Holy Spirit cannot dwell in unclean vessel.

Isaiah 52:11

Depart! Depart! Go out from there, Touch no unclean thing; Go out from the midst of her, Be clean, You who bear the vessels of the LORD. (NKJ)

This is very dreadful especially if the individual was highly anointed and doing the will of God. They end up becoming empty vessel and void without God. Their prayer life stops, their communion with God stops, they stop reading and meditating on the Word of God and completely driven out of the presence of God.

6. Their temple becomes now the temple of demons. Since the Holy Spirit has left, the devil now takes control. Demon of lust comes in, demon of anger, demon of bitterness, demon of lies, demon of seduction, demon of masturbation, demon of ties of relational bonds and the like. The temple becomes the temple of the devil, a place where devil now rules freely.

7. The joy of the Lord will be taken. Once the joy is taken, it becomes a life of pain and bitterness, a life of problems in and out. Everything will start to shake in your life. The Lord will make sure there is nothing you will enjoy, for the scriptures says that there is no peace for the wicked.

Isaiah 48:22

"There is no peace," says the LORD, "for the wicked." (NKJ)

Isaiah 57:21

There is no peace," says my God, "for the wicked." (NKJ)

You will never find your peace, whether in your pursuit of studies, in your job and day to day activities, you will be laboring in vain and you will never enjoy the fruit of your labor! You will labor but someone else will eat. God will make sure your whores will eat it and you will remain empty handed.

8. Your respect, honor and dignity will be taken. In other words, your crown of life will be taken. The crown of glory the Lord had put in your life will go. You will become so useless and a vessel of men's or women's manipulation. Sex before marriage takes your dignity. Once your dignity is gone, wherever you go, it shall be written in your face that you are a vessel of manipulation. You will become more vulnera-

ble to more abuse by men and women. People will misuse you, degrade you, destroy your very being, because you sold your dignity looking for pleasure.

> *Proverbs 5: 8 Remove your way far from her,*
> *And do not go near the door of her house,*
> *9 Lest you give your honor to others,*
> *And your years to the cruel one;*
> *10 Lest aliens be filled with your wealth,*
> *And your labors go to the house of a foreigner;*
> *11 And you mourn at last,*
> *When your flesh and your body are consumed,*
> *12 And say: "How I have hated instruction,*
> *And my heart despised correction!*
> *13 I have not obeyed the voice of my teachers,*
> *Nor inclined my ear to those who instructed me!*
> *14 I was on the verge of total ruin,*
> *In the midst of the assembly and congregation." (NKJ)*

The Bible says many great men have fallen because of her, in actual sense the Bible bespeaks of fornication and adultery. Many servants of God have fallen to this sin and the power of God have left them. They lost their honor and dignity.

If you are a man, the Lord will take the crown of respect he gave you to be the leader in the house. If you end up getting married your wife will rule over you, because every moment she will set her eyes on you, she won't be able to see the crown of life and the authority of God as the head, why, because the Lord took it. So now you have to know some of the reason why your wife may not be giving you respect as the head of the house, think twice, you might have sold cheaply your crown of life with that whore on the streets, or that college girl or that party girl before you got married.

God can never be fooled, whatsoever a man sows shall he also reap. Sex before marriage may seem pleasurable for the moment, but I promise you, God will for sure make you see the consequences of it in your life.

9. Some ended up in this act and they got tied spiritually and closed up. To men, they can lose their manhood and never be infatuated with a lady again, especially the problem will rise in marriage. To a lady, your womb can be closed never to give birth.

10. Marriage problems. Since you got accessed to satanic demons through the people you slept around with, if your partner sleeps with you, they will see the devil who you are married to not them. Some people have ended up being married to the devil and unclean spirits through these acts. That defile them when they sleep and when they wake up, they are not themselves. This problem can become persistent in marriage and lead to marriage breakups. You begin to wonder why your husband doesn't like you, because when he sleeps with you, he realizes you belong to somebody else who is your spiritual husband. Many are in bondage because of this!

11. Leads to multiple spiritual husbands and wives. The first person you have sex with out of wedlock becomes your first wife or husband. So, begin to count how many husband and wives you have right now! When Jesus saw the Samaritan woman at the well, she told her you have heard five husbands and the one you now have is not your husband. How is it possible for the Samaritan woman to have five husbands yet she was not married? In actual sense, before the eyes of Jesus, every of the men she slept with were recorded as her husband. Be careful, on the judgement day you will be surprised how many wives and husbands you had yet God ordained you to have only one!

John 4:18
for you have had five husbands, and the one whom you now have is not your husband; in that you spoke truly." (NKJ)

Repent and prepare the way of the Lord. if this have found you, cry for mercies of the Lord, repent seriously before the Lord and seek for help and deliverance.

Eleven

MARRIAGE IS NOT A SOLUTION TO LUST

Marriage is not a solution to lust, solution to lust is dying at Calvary. Sex is meant for sharing of love and unity between couples which leads to children being born.

Sex is not a tool of fulfillment of lust.

Sex is a process of discovering your partner well by accessing their spirit and their soul.

It takes diligence to want to know somebody, it takes gentleness, it takes patience. The Bible says then Isaac knew his wife and bore a son. Why does the Bible use the word "knew" instead of sex? Sex is an intertwining process, where the two becomes ONE. How can two becomes one? It is a process of soul to spirit exchange, a sensitive place which shouldn't be done by just anybody but your legally wedded wife or husband.

The devil have really mis taught our generation about sex. To think that sex is all about excitement and fulfillment of lust. Sex comes with a responsibility; to our young people, sex can either build you or destroy you. Sex is destructive when it is not used according to its intended purpose.

LESSONS ABOUT SEX:

Sex determines the status of the children to be born. Your children can either be clean or unclean through sex.

Sex is not a joke, it is not a tool to be misused, it is not to be experimented before the right time in marriage.

Sex before marriage takes a man's honor and authority. That's why our men who are supposed to be leaders beginning from household, are following behind the tail, for a prostitute somewhere ran away with their honor.

Sex before marriage makes men weak and useless and it makes women object of misuse.

Sex before marriage destroys a woman's self-image. Then begin to live to please others than living to please God.
These is why many are struggling with low self-esteem, which leads to use of make ups, miniskirts and tight trousers.

Finally sex must be done according to the way God design it to be.

HOW TO KEEP YOURSELF FROM SEXUAL TEMPTATION BEFORE MARRIAGE.

We live in a time where keeping sexual purity is not easy. However sexual purity before marriage is a desirable trait, many end up not having it by the time they get married. One young lady from Philippines whom I disciple who happened to be in a relationship, asked me about this important question. How can a young man keep themselves from sexual temptations? This section will cover ways to keep yourself from sexual temptation while courting and awaiting marriage.

Do not awaken love before its time.
Song of Solomon 8:4
Promise me, O women of Jerusalem, not to awaken love until the time is right. Young Women of Jerusalem. (NLT)

There is always big excitement of getting into a relationship and you want to experience many things. There is need of walking very carefully especially if the commitment to marriage is not yet determined. Have seen many young people entering a relationship but they expect to marry ten years later. There are somethings that are better not experimented until the right time. The fact of you entering a love relationship with a person of your opposite sex is enough of a challenge. It will awaken every feelings and emotions which has been quiet all along and if you are not ready to balance the emotions that comes with relationships, mistake is expected to happen.

Have seen people who are truly born again and enter a relationship which end up in fornication before marriage. No matter how saved you are, never forget that the flesh never get saved only your spirit does. We must be careful how we deal and react with the flesh.

It is important to avoid love language during courting season. Calling yourself using love language will awaken you and it will be difficult to bring down the fire that is already lit. In the Book of Songs of Solomon, it says I adjure you daughters of Zion to awaken not or stir up love until it pleases. There is a time for everything under the Sun, there are matters that are better left or done at the appropriate time. It is dangerous to awaken emotions that cannot be quenched within a period. Wisdom calls for careful consideration of time and to avoid unnecessary mistakes that will be costly.

It is not advisable to expose your relationship to the public when plans of marriage are not under the seen. There are many people who want to expose their relationship to the world and show people how romantic they are before thinking about the marriage date. Exposing your relationship to the public will put you into many challenges and temptations. You will become the target for Satan, jealous friends and public ridicule. If you can keep your relationship secret between the two of you or people who are very close to you, it will be better. You can reveal your relationship when you are sure that marriage is near.

Guard Your Eyes

Luke 11:34

"Your eye is like a lamp that provides light for your body. When your eye is healthy, your whole body is filled with light. But when it is unhealthy, your body is filled with darkness. (NLT)

God made us in such a way that our body naturally react with what we see. This is the reason why the Bible says guard your eyes for it is the lamp to your body. If your eyes are full of light, then your body will be of light and if your eyes is full of darkness then your body will be dark. What you see and watch matters if you want to maintain your sexual purity. In a world dominated with sexual perversion and images that allures people into sexual sin, you will need to make deliberate decision to stay apart.

Today, even the movies people watch has sexual insinuation that can slowly enter you to sin. What you see will affect the way your body reacts.

There is also something about the eyes that it never get satisfied. Our generation today is feeding on images that have darkened their souls and they are never satisfied. Watch what you see and engage in healthy activities that can bring light to your body.

Proverbs 27:20

Hell and Destruction are never full; So the eyes of man are never satisfied.

Fasting and Prayer.

1 Corinthians 9:27

But I discipline my body and bring it into subjection, lest, when I have preached to others, I myself should become disqualified. (NKV)

There is no way to overcome sexual temptation if you don't fast and pray. Many Christians have become the lazy kind and expect to overcome temptations without fasting. You must develop a culture of personal fasting to keep your body in check. Don't fast because somebody has told you to fast but consider fasting as part of your Christian life.

If you can overcome temptation of food, you can overcome any other temptations.

Avoid being in Wrong Places

Proverbs 7:6 For at the window of my house
I looked through my lattice,
7 And saw among the simple,
I perceived among the youths,
A young man devoid of understanding,
8 Passing along the street near her corner;
And he took the path to her house
9 In the twilight, in the evening,
In the black and dark night.
10 And there a woman met him,
With the attire of a harlot, and a crafty heart.
11 She was loud and rebellious,
Her feet would not stay at home. (NKV)

Many people have landed into unnecessary problems for being in a wrong place at a wrong time. The book of Proverbs talk of a young man roaming on the streets near the house of a promiscuous woman in the evening time when it is approaching darkness. The question that comes is what was he doing there at that time? Why roam near the house of a promiscuous woman and especially when it is approaching darkness? Why are you going to visit the house of your partner when you know they live alone? Why going to segregated places where only few people can see the two of you and expect not to fall into sin? Why join that birthday party when alcohol will be part of the day? Why stay late chatting when you are supposed to be back at your home? The young man in the book of proverb was caught up in a mess he didn't expect for roaming in wrong places. You must be careful of the kind of friends that you have near you. Sometimes you can tell from the signals these friends gives you. There are some people who should not be visited easily. You may need to accompany yourself with somebody else when going to visit certain people.

There are people who have ended up being raped while going for a home Bible Study. If you happen to go to a Bible study in the house of a single lady or man and nobody else is a round, don't enter that house. Better wait from outside until a third party comes in. Application of wisdom can truly save you from costly mistakes.

1 Corinthians 15:33

Do not be deceived: "Evil company corrupts good habits." (NKJ)

Twelve

THE REASON BEHIND THE CHASING

What is the reason young man, you are chasing after that woman or girl? Is it because of her miniskirt, open chest, her looks, her level of education, her material wealth, her pictures of attention and advertisements on Facebook and social media or her job?

There are many unmarried men chasing after women for very wrong reasons. Not only do they chase after them, they want to explore places they are not permitted to explore.

I started chasing after my wife when I saw the radiance of Christ in her , when I saw the power of the indwelling Christ what it had done on her life , when I realized the hope of glory Jesus Christ lived in her , I automatically fell in love with her . I knew I couldn't be wrong for the reason of choosing her was Christ, the Rock of my own foundation, the Christ Jesus the Lord and the Hope of my life, was on her life and Jesus on her life drew me to her.

The beauty of Christ made it possible, for I had first fallen in love with Christ and Christ made her more appealing to be my wife. No matter what many voices and manly opinion that came against her, couldn't make me doubt the choice I have made, for I knew the best choice somebody can ever make is to involve Christ on it.

We wanted to honor God with our lives, and we had to maintain our chastity till after marriage. There was no careless arousing neither mouth to mouth kissing, for Jesus had to be the foundation of our union in marriage. The first kiss we had mouth to mouth was on our marriage day when we were joined as husband and wife.

Thirteen

FOUNDATION ISSUES TO DEAL WITH BEFORE MARRIAGE

Psalm 11:3
if the foundations are destroyed, what can the righteous do? (NKJ)

Foundation issues: things people ignore but becomes a reality after marriage.
To the singles, those that have intent of getting married and even those in courting with intent of getting married, don't ignore foundational issues.

Foundational issues are more than able to kick you out of your marriage life.
Foundational issues is more than able to make your marriage depressing.
Foundational issue is more than able to make you lose interest in your partner.

Foundational issue is more than able to tear family apart.
Foundational issue is more than able to make marriage unfulfilling .

Even though many do ignore these issues for some are too sensitive to be opened or dealt with, it is more important to deal with these issues especially before marriage.

WHAT ARE SOME OF THESE ISSUES?

1. Someone who was raped as a child but was never healed properly. The damage that was done in the spirit of that person human doctors cannot cure only the Lord can. No amount of counseling can cure this, only the power of God. Many are entering into marriage when they are deeply wounded. There was a seed of destruction that the devil had already planted that will make their marriage life miserable. A person who has been raped may not have interest to do with sex in marriage and the normal person on the other hand may have interest and this can lead to big conflicts that can lead the partner to seek for satisfaction outside of marriage.

2. Witchcraft. If you grew in a family where witchcraft was prevalent and probably your parents or forefathers largely participated on it. You need to seek for deliverance to be disconnected from those foundation for them never to follow you up in your marriage. Some of these things follow people even in marriage and you begin to wonder why your partner is behaving the way they are behaving because they are being controlled somewhere else.

3. Bond of relationship from previous emotional relationship. These bonds can be so strong especially if sex was involved. You can be spiritually united with the other person wherever they are. These can be chaotic and follow you even inside marriage.

For instance, you will find a man or woman refraining from sexual intercourse with their partner for he or she feels the presence of a third party between them every time they come into contact sexually.

4.

Spiritual covenants with demons. Some people do go for consultation in the houses of mediums or witches and they are made to have covenants with demons, even get married to demons. These demons can include succubus and incubus. Demons that can claim an individual that they are married to them. These demons will fight for you to stay single and not to settle in marriage and if married, will fight to tear the family apart.

In our generation today with the sexual pollution and demonic activities in the social media and internet , majority of people are in bondage of this demonic activities .
Some will confess that they can recognize the presence of a third party who comes to sleep with them on bed and they wake up in the morning completely wet. They know for sure they had sexual intercourse with a demon. These continue until it becomes a habit and this individual is in bondage, they know not how to come out of. This do affect even married couples.

This is a big problem that is affecting many marriages, and many have gone into silence, for they are ashamed to speak of their experiences. I want to tell you today, shame the devil and expose his works, the Blood of Jesus is still on the business of setting men free from the bondage of Satan.

> ***Ephesians 5:11 And have no fellowship with the unfruitful works of darkness, but rather expose them. (NKJ)***
> ***1 John 3:8 He who sins is of the devil, for the devil has sinned from the beginning. For this purpose the Son of God was manifested, that He might destroy the works of the devil. (NKJ)***

Fourteen

BENEFITS OF HOLY MATRIMONY

Our society today doesn't see it wrong when a man and woman cohabits together and lives in sin, but demons of hell will break loose when couples choose the right way in honoring their marriage before God by wedding matrimony.

The day I decided to wed my wife and have a Holy Matrimony is the time all kind of hell broke loose :

People who wanted me to live in sin came along.

Generational strongholds woke up.

Strife and jealousy broke loose and all manner of chaos.

I thank God for those who stood with me on the process.

Reasons why the devil doesn't want you to officially marry:

1. Children born out of wedlock are completely cursed and will continue living in bondage of generational strongholds. While children born in a sanctified marriage are blessed. Why? Because the marriage sanctify them from the womb.
1 Corinthians 7:14 For the unbelieving husband is sanctified by the

wife, and the unbelieving wife is sanctified by the husband; otherwise your children would be unclean, but now they are holy. (NKJ)

2. Whoever lives in fornication is a devil's property. Your ticket is already in hell while you are on earth. It doesn't matter how many years the two have lived together and how many children the two has given birth to, fornication is fornication before the eyes of God.

    Some have been living in sin for years, even became church leaders but still living in sin. Hell shall you wake up in if you fail to repent. Marriage bed is honorable before God and marriage must be done in a proper way as God instituted it. Children must be raised in godly environment!

    Hebrews 13:4 Marriage is honorable among all, and the bed undefiled; but fornicators and adulterers God will judge. (NKJ)

3. The blessing from the altar. When the elders pray for you at the altar on your wedding day, there are blessings you receive from God that will help sustain your marriage. You make a public declaration that you have involved the Heaven backup and anything that will try to attack and separate your unity with your spouse will become God's enemy too. We always need a strong army to win, make sure you involve the armies of Heaven in your marriage.

Proverbs 18:22 He who finds a wife finds a good thing, And obtains favor from the LORD. (NKJ)

Testimony

When me and my wife are faced with a challenge we always go back to the foundation of our relationship.

When I tell people that me and my wife never met face to face until two weeks to our wedding at the Altar many don't believe.

It was faith that moved mountains for us. It was faith that made our long-distance relationship to work. It was faith that made us know each other not by the way we look but how our hearts and soul looked like. God by His grace intertwined us that sometimes we could dream the same dream while she is in Kenya while am in U.S.

I remember coming to her telling her, dear I had a dream and she will be like I had a dream too and after sharing our dreams it turns to be the same thing.

Faith moved mountains for us against all obstacles we faced, for who can understand faith for faith believes on what is not seen.

To our youths trusting God for marriage partner do not underestimate the one the Lord has chosen for you.

There was a time I prayed for so many years for God to bring to my life and Ministry somebody with a special gift that can work together with my calling, but little did I know my own wife possessed that gift. Over suddenly this gift begun unraveling. Am deeply grateful for what the Lord is doing in our lives.

Fifteen

MESSAGE TO OUR SINGLE PARENTS

No matter how strong you are as a mother and even financially stable, you cannot be a father to that child. No matter how strong you are as a father and even financially stable, you cannot be a mother to that child.

They're aspects of a mother a child can only learn from a mother and they're aspects of a father a child can only learn from a father. When I talk of a father and a mother am talking about real mothers and fathers who have what it takes to be both.

In today's society, the devil has deceived many that all a child needs is themselves not a family .To parents , the best gift you can ever give to your child is a family ; where mother and father are actively playing their role in raising that child .

Our fathers today don't know how to be father even in marriage because there was no father in their lives and our mothers don't not know what it takes to be a mother because there was no mother in their lives.

The incomplete generation our society is raising is what has brought gender complexity. Where men don't know they are men and women don't know there are women because there is a missing place in their lives.

We are raising a grieving generation, full of bitterness, misery and hatred because the responsible parties didn't see the need of acting as adults who brought a child to the world. That child doesn't not need your money, neither your child support they need your presence.

To our single ladies who act with attitude who sees the need of a child more than the need of a man in their lives, that child doesn't need you alone, they need the father too who played the role of their existence.

Let's fight to bring order to our society and prove to the devil that indeed marriage works, the institution first created by God indeed works and that institution is meant to raise godly children.

It takes two to raise godly children and to bring a balance to a child's life.

Parents, that child needs both of you. Don't think about sex before thinking about responsibility and don't think about sex before marriage. For God will held every parent into judgement of not playing their roles as parents to the life of their children.

Deuteronomy 6:6-7 And these words that I command you today shall be on your heart. You shall teach them diligently to your children and shall talk of them when you sit in your house, and when you walk by the way, and when you lie down, and when you rise.

Sixteen

BE CAUTIOUS IN RELATIONSHIPS

The truth is that there is no Christian boyfriend or girlfriend, those doors have indeed opened the gateway for the devil to infiltrate the church with this lie from the world.

In category of the church among believers, the Bible clearly stipulate that you shall call them your brothers and sisters in the Lord.

Those young men or women who are not yet married, should relate with people of their opposite sex in the church as brothers and sisters in the Lord; the friendship should be based on that.

And if it reaches a time a brother in the Lord want to enter into a meaningful relationship with the purpose of marriage , first they should pray and wait on the Lord and if they have a leading to a certain sister, they should approach the sister cautiously.

If they find out that the sister is already in another relationship with another man or engaged to another person, they should respect that and not move forward. For God is not an author of confusion to lead you to such a person.

If the sister agree that the two are of the same mind, they can both pray for the will of God about it. If they find out that their minds are set up for a long-term meaningful relationship to marriage, they should approach their Pastor for further direction.

1 Thessalonians 4: 3 For this is the will of God, your sanctification: that you should abstain from sexual immorality; 4 that each of you should know how to possess his own vessel in sanctification and honor, 5 not in passion of lust, like the Gentiles who do not know God; 6 that no one should take advantage of and defraud his brother in this matter, because the Lord is the avenger of all such, as we also forewarned you and testified. 7 For God did not call us to uncleanness, but in holiness. 8 Therefore he who rejects this does not reject man, but God, who has also given us His Holy Spirit.

9 But concerning brotherly love you have no need that I should write to you, for you yourselves are taught by God to love one another; 10 and indeed you do so toward all the brethren who are in all Macedonia. But we urge you, brethren, that you increase more and more; 11 that you also aspire to lead a quiet life, to mind your own business, and to work with your own hands, as we commanded you, 12 that you may walk properly toward those who are outside, and that you may lack nothing.(NKJ)

Seventeen

DON'T WAIT FOR HER IN A DREAM

If you are a young man praying for a wife, do not expect God to send the wife through dreams, instead the devil can send you one.

When it comes to marriage God is very practical. There are people praying for a wife but instead of waiting for the wife to appear in the physical they are waiting in the spiritual. Prayer is a spiritual substance and prayer about marriage partner God will surely answer in the physical.

There are brothers in the Lord that have been waiting for years for God to send their wives through dreams, they have become too spiritual until they lost understanding that something's needs to happen in the physical.

There is category of people whom also the enemy deceived by bringing someone to them in a dream, when they went to approach the person, they came to realize either the person is already married or engaged to someone else. These people will even claim using the name of God that the Lord has spoken to them, even when the other individual may not want to enter a relationship with them, they may insist in the basis of the dream they saw.

They also don't know that there is a possibility they might have been admiring the person in their thoughts to the extent the person now appears on their dreams and in real facts they will be led with their own fleshly appetite but not the Spirit of God to approach the individual .These have caused many to be hurt in the church and broken friendship.

The Lord, the God of the Bible, is not an author of confusion and if you pray to Him for a wife, do not expect God to send the wife to you in the complicated spiritual world of dreams but in the physical. Just as Abraham's servant prayed for Isaac's wife at the well, God brought her at the well where she could be seen.

Genesis 24:12 Then he said, "O Lord God of my master Abraham, please give me success this day, and show kindness to my master Abraham. 13 Behold, here I stand by the well of water, and the daughters of the men of the city are coming out to draw water. 14Now let it be that the young woman to whom I say, 'Please let down your pitcher that I may drink,' and she says, 'Drink, and I will also give your camels a drink'—let her be the one You have appointed for Your servant Isaac. And by this I will know that You have shown kindness to my master."

15 And it happened, before he had finished speaking, that behold, Rebekah, who was born to Bethuel, son of Milcah, the wife of Nahor, Abraham's brother, came out with her pitcher on her shoulder. 16 Now the young woman was very beautiful to behold, a virgin; no man had known her. And she went down to the well, filled her pitcher, and came up. 17 And the servant ran to meet her and said, "Please let me drink a little water from your pitcher." 18 So she said, "Drink, my lord." Then she quickly let her pitcher down to her hand, and gave him a drink. 19 And when she had finished giving him a drink, she said, "I will draw water for your camels also, until they have finished drinking." 20 Then she quickly emptied her pitcher into the trough, ran back to the well to draw water, and drew for all his camels. 21 And the man, wondering at her, remained silent so as to know whether the Lord had made his journey prosperous or not.

22 So it was, when the camels had finished drinking, that the man took a golden nose ring weighing half a shekel, and two bracelets for her wrists weighing ten shekels of gold, 23 and said, "Whose daughter are you? Tell me, please, is there room in your father's house for us to lodge?"

24 So she said to him, "I am the daughter of Bethuel, Milcah's son, whom she bore to Nahor." 25 Moreover she said to him, "We have both straw and feed enough, and room to lodge."

*26 Then the man bowed down his head and worshiped the Lord. 27 And he said, **"Blessed be the Lord God of my master Abraham, who has not forsaken His mercy and His truth toward my master. As for me, being on the way, the Lord led me to the house of my master's brethren."** 28 So the young woman ran and told her mother's household these things. (NKJ)*

Eighteen

THE GLORY OF A WIFE IS HER HUSBAND

The glory of a wife is on her husband. If you disgrace your husband, you will disgrace yourself and you won't shine. To our women, your shining and uplifting depend on how you treat and relate with your husband since he is your glory. Respect the glory if you want to reach far. If you dishonor your husband, you will trample on the glory and the glory will disgrace you.

> *1 Corinthians 11:7 For a man ought not to cover his head, since he is the image and glory of God, but woman is the glory of man.*

Glory is meant to redefine you and make you better before the eyes of men and God. The big mistake many do is trying to fight with the Glory or trying to disgrace the Glory. As a woman, it is critical to understand that your blessing is hidden in the loins of your husband. How you treat your husband, how you talk to your husband, how you respect and honor your husband will contribute to your shining. The better you treat your husband the better you will receive acknowledgements and excellence in what you do. Sarah received excellence as a mother to nations because she treated her husband well.

Your husband may not be earning and bringing home the same amount of money you bring but still honor him. He can be alcoholic and lack in many things but still honor him. Remember he is your glory. Glory is meant to be respected if you want to see good result coming out of it. The same way the Glory of man is God; in other words for a man to shine and succeed, he must learn to honor God with his life. Acknowledge God wherever he goes and preach the Kingdom of God. The more a man honors God, the more they receive promotion from God but the moment a man dishonor God with their life is the moment they will receive demotion from God.

Marry someone you deeply respect and honor or else you will find it difficult to submit. If the man is not worth your respect, don't marry him.

May God give you grace and wisdom to understand this section to help you live in harmony together with your husband. When we come to clear understanding of our role and place in marriage, it makes it easier to live in harmony and joy.

Nineteen

GOOD CHARACTER

Good character is what builds a family but when good character is lacking in a Christian family, it can put the marriage in danger and even tore it part.

It is not about material wealth the partners may have or level of education but if Jesus is in the marriage accompanied with godly character towards each other that marriage will work, but if one partner has bad attitude it will tear the marriage apart and it can end up to be a bitter marriage like the one of David and Saul's daughter Michal.

At first Michal loved David and desired to get married to David *(1 Samuel 18:20 Now Saul's daughter Michal loved David. And they told Saul, and the thing pleased him.)* but she failed in character in respect to the man God had given to her as a husband. Therefore she was not able to fulfill key responsibility on the life of David, according to the Bible she remained barren the rest of her life for she failed in character.

2 Samuel 6: 20 Then David returned to bless his household. And Michal the daughter of Saul came out to meet David, and said, "How glorious was the king of Israel today, uncovering himself today in the eyes of the maids of his servants, as one of the base fellows shamelessly uncovers himself!"

21 So David said to Michal, "It was before the Lord, who chose me instead of your father and all his house, to appoint me ruler over the people of the Lord, over Israel. Therefore I will play music before the Lord. 22 And I will be even more undignified than this, and will be humble in my own sight. But as for the maidservants of whom you have spoken, by them I will be held in honor."
23 Therefore Michal the daughter of Saul had no children to the day of her death. (NKJ)

Proverbs 21:9 Better to dwell in a corner of a housetop, Than in a house shared with a contentious woman. (NKJ)

On the other hand, we see Abigail the wife of Nabal because of her exceptional character and respect she showed towards David by serving him and his servants and the fear of the Lord she demonstrated toward David even before David was made King of Israel, finally made her to gain favor before the eyes of David and David took her as a wife after her husband died.

1 Samuel 25:3 The name of the man was Nabal, and the name of his wife Abigail. And she was a woman of good understanding and beautiful appearance; but the man was harsh and evil in his doings. He was of the house of Caleb. (NKJ)

1 Samuel 25:18 Then Abigail made haste and took two hundred loaves of bread, two skins of wine, five sheep already dressed, five seahs of roasted grain, one hundred clusters of raisins, and two hundred cakes of figs, and loaded them on donkeys. (NKJ)

There are people who have remained barren, in ministry or family because they failed in character , may bad character not rob you of your destiny , learn to humble yourself before the Lord and even spiritual authority God has put above you beginning from the house .

Character traits to work on

*2 Peter 1: 5 But also for this very reason, giving all diligence, add to your faith **virtue**, to virtue **knowledge**, 6 to knowledge **self-control**, to self-control **perseverance**, to perseverance **godliness**, 7 to godliness **brotherly kindness**, and to brotherly kindness **love**. 8 For if these things are yours and abound, you will be **neither barren nor unfruitful in the knowledge of our Lord Jesus Christ**. 9 For he who lacks these things is shortsighted, even to blindness, and has forgotten that he was cleansed from his old sins. (NKJ)*

Virtue

Virtue is defined as a behavior showing high moral standards. It is important to ask yourself the kind of behavior you show around and how you carry yourself. What can people say about you? How do you dress when you leave home? Do you dress in a godly manner? How do you talk with people? Do you show respect and honor while talking with people? Virtue walks with us and is seen in how we interact with other people daily. Virtue is a key character of showing the image of Jesus Christ in our lives. It shows that we are following the footsteps of Jesus Christ by living the way He lived, talking the way He talked and loving the way He loved.

Knowledge

The Bible says that my people perish because of lack of knowledge. It is important to make a deliberate decision to acquire knowledge of marriage according to the Bible. Choosing to read this book is one step of showing that you want to acquire knowledge. Knowledge help us to make wise decisions and avoid many problems. There are many situations that will occur in marriage where good knowledge will be able to solve them. It is important to spend time to hear the mind of God concerning marriage before entering one. It becomes hard for people to submit to the will of God when they later come to realize how God thinks concerning different situations.

Self-Control

2 Timothy 1:7 For God has not given us a spirit of fear, but of power and of love and of a sound mind. (NKJ)

Self-control is a character you strongly develop through your personal walk with God and your relationship with the Holy Spirit. The more you relate with God the more you develop the power of self-control. You will find yourself in places where you are able to control your desires and emotions. In many occasions you will have to learn how to fast and pray. Fasting is one of the major ways of developing this key character in life.

Perseverance.

There are many things you will see in marriage that will require a heart of perseverance. In marriage you will meet with a woman or man who grew up in a completely different environment and raised differently. In every house a child is raised with a different background and this plays part in their upbringing and the character that embodies the individual. In marriage you will be able to see behaviors that you may not like in your partner. It will call for the heart of perseverance to keep going. May God give you a heart of perseverance to endure every test that will come to shake your marriage life.

Godliness.

Hebrews 12:14
Pursue peace with all people, and holiness, without which no one will see the Lord (NJV)
1Timothy 4:8
For bodily exercise profits a little, but godliness is profitable for all things, having promise of the life that now is and of that which is to come.
(NJV)

Godliness as part of marriage is the reason the Bible speaks of keeping the marital bed undefiled. The couples must live true to one another and stay faithful to their marital vows they made before God. They must stay away from relationships that can lead to compromise to that vow. Remember God is the third union between couples. What keeps God in the marriage is the level of godliness. You want the presence of God to preserve your marriage against the avengers, demons and attacks. Fighting for godliness is fighting to keep God's fire active between the marriage. The fire of God keeps the marriage going and give grace from time to time to overcome different challenges that comes along.

Hebrews 13:4 Marriage is honorable among all, and the bed undefiled; but fornicators and adulterers God will judge. (NKJ)

Brotherly Kindness

Extend your generosity to others. Treat others well by meeting them at the point of their needs. Cover the naked when you see one, feed the hungry and reach out to the needs of the orphans and widows. Life becomes enjoyable when you realize it is not all about yourself. You have something to share with world. Spread kindness to the world and show them the power of the love of God.

James 1:27
Pure and undefiled religion before God and the Father is this: to visit orphans and widows in their trouble, and to keep oneself unspotted from the world. (NKJ)

Love

Sometimes love expressed is much more than love concealed in the heart. However the FATHER loved humanity in his heart, he had to express that love to us through Jesus Christ. Jesus proved to us that the Father loved us, that when we were yet sinners, the Lord died for us.

Let us not conceal the Gift of love in our hearts but express it by deeds. Let us not to be stingy with our love but express it to one another that even non-believers can see our unity in Christ. And this goes even to family and marriage relationships, many marriages are hurting today because the partners have concealed their love to their own hearts.

Love must be expressed through action and deeds, not through frowning and silence. Many people are hurting today in marriage because pride is killing them, they can't show love to their partner, because they expect their partner to show love first. Then it ends up to a fight, distant separation, lack of proper communication and ambiguity in marriage. Where people argue all the time over little things.

If you are married, when have you reached to your partner to help them even work out household duty?

If you are a man, when have you remembered that even your wife needs rest and go and clean the kitchen and utensils, cook and prepare the food on the table? My dad taught me a lesson I will never forget that finished my pride. He could cook on my behalf, prepare the table, bring you a class of water or juice, while the son is just seated.

Most of a time staying with my dad, he did prepare for me breakfast out of love, telling me breakfast is an important meal even the days I used to fast and running away from breakfast, my dad could bring it to me already made.

If you are a lady when have you loved your husband and be infatuated with him according to Proverbs 5:18?

> *Proverbs 5: 18 Let your fountain be blessed,*
> *And rejoice with the wife of your youth.*
> *19 As a loving deer and a graceful doe,*
> *Let her breasts satisfy you at all times;*
> *And always be enraptured with her love.(NKJ)*

When last did you hug your partner and told him or her that you love them? Love must be expressed, and it will make marriage lovely and cover all sins.

Love will cover all petty, petty mistakes your partner may try to do. But if you fail to express it, this will lead to those marriages that are dry, no proper communication, no smiling, no prayer, no Bible study together and it reached a time that those two partners will have to sleep on different bedrooms or bed.

When it reached where partners separate to different bed, then know your marriage has reached a bad state. You will lose spiritual connection with your husband or wife; you won't act no more as two to build the marriage up but as one to tear the marriage down.

There is something that happens when partners have contact with one another in bed. First, there is peace and security, second, they keep themselves warm, third they bond in one spirit and forth it brings ease of communication. But today the modern society can even teach you to sleep on different bedrooms this is tricky and it is a lie from the pit of darkness to tear marriages down and when that happened the partners will lose bond with one another and confusion and misunderstanding with come.

You won't be able to recognize your partner especially when they are in need because you are not bonded together in physical contact. Even in the Bible, it says when David was old, there was need to look for a beautiful maiden in the land of Israel, not to come and have sex with him but just to sleep with him on the same bed and keep him warm. This is how important partners sleeping together on the same bed. Practice these things in your marriage if married and your marriage will work out, for love expressed is much better than love concealed in the human heart! Always be the first to express it out of a genuine heart and the other will follow.

> *1 Peter 3:1 Wives, likewise, be submissive to your own husbands, that even if some do not obey the word, they, without a word, may be won by the conduct of their wives, (NKJ)*

> *1 Kings 1: 1 Now King David was old, advanced in years; and they put covers on him, but he could not get warm. 2 Therefore his servants said to him, "Let a young woman, a virgin, be sought for our lord the king, and let her stand before the king, and let her care for him; and let her lie in your bosom, that our lord the king may be warm." 3 So they sought for a lovely young woman throughout all the territory of Israel, and found Abishag the Shunammite, and brought her to the king. 4 The young woman was very lovely; and she cared for the king, and served him; but the king did not know her. (NKJ)*

Twenty

ABOUT THE AUTHOR

    LENIN O. WERE is a husband, father and pastor of Restoration of the Tent of David Church. Called to the ministry at a tender age where he entered the service of the Lord. He has served in the church in different levels from being a youth usher, youth intercessory leader, Bible study leader and was ordained as a Minister of the Gospel at age twenty-three.

    At age 31 he was ordained as Pastor and now serves in pastoral calling. He has been a blessing to many through his gift in teaching, healing, leadership training and counsel. He now aspires to bring the message of the Cross Internationally and impact nations of the world with the powerful Gospel of Jesus Christ.

    Being raised in a broken home, he aims at bringing hope to marriages in the brick of breaking, restoring children back to their parents and being a father to many.

www.ingramcontent.com/pod-product-compliance
Lightning Source LLC
Chambersburg PA
CBHW040002110526
44587CB00001BA/25